ENGLISH DRESS IN THE AGE OF S̶H̶A̶K̶E̶S̶P̶E̶A̶R̶E̶

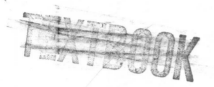

ENGLISH DRESS IN THE AGE OF
SHAKESPEARE

DATE DUE			

English Dress in the Age of Shakespeare

BY VIRGINIA A. LA MAR

FOLGER BOOKS

Published by
THE FOLGER SHAKESPEARE LIBRARY

LC 79-91465
ISBN 0-918016-31-2 (previously ISBN 0-8139-0088-3)
ISBN 0-918016-18-5 (Series)

Printed in the United States of America

ENGLISH dress during the age of Shakespeare reflected the vitality and high spirits of the period. The growth of England as a world power, the increase in trade and prosperity, and the political stability created by Queen Elizabeth's shrewd policies, all helped to develop a spirit of self-confidence. One result of this exuberance was an increase in the taste for fine raiment and an indulgence in magnificent clothing which make the Elizabethan age one of the most gorgeously dressed periods in the island's history.

Although the upper class and even the great merchants of earlier eras had also dressed in rich and colorful fabrics, the sixteenth century saw an elaboration in dress that had not been common. In keeping with the doctrine that everyone was born to a certain station ordained by heaven and should content himself with his lot, however humble, sumptuary laws had traditionally prescribed the degrees of luxury permissible to each class. For example, folk under the rank of a knight's eldest son were prohibited from wearing satin, damask, taffeta, and similar rich attire. Queen Elizabeth retained legislation to this end, but the power and wealth of the middle class increased during her reign to such a point that the previous regulations had to be relaxed; in a new statute of 1580 they were modified to allow a certain degree of finery to those who could afford it. A parallel may be seen in the attitudes of the Puritan elders of New England, who attempted to discourage the wearing of fine clothes by similar laws in the first decades of colonization. Eventually, however, they had to give up the effort because prosperity in their flocks stimulated an irrepressible desire for finery.

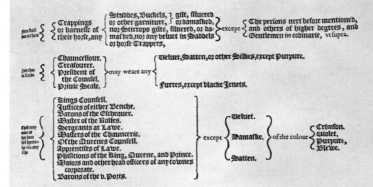

Note that her Maiesties meaning is not, by this order, to forbid in any person the wearing of fylke buttons, the facing of Coates, Clokes, Hattes, and Cappes, for comlynesse onely with Taffata, Grograyne, Veluet, or other fylke as is commonly vfed.

Note alfo that the meaning of this order, is not to prohibite a feruant frō wearing of any cognifance of his mafter, or Henchmen, Heralds, Purfeuantes at armes, Runners at Iuftes, Turnaies, or fuch martiall feates, and fuch as weare apparell giuen by the Queene, and fuch as fhall haue licence from the Queene for the fame.

❧ *Womens apparrell.*

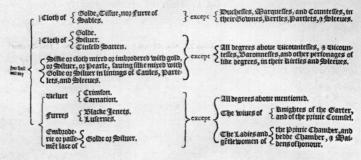

Illus. 1. One of four pages of a proclamation against excess in apparel issued June 15, 1574. Throughout her reign Queen Elizabeth issued such proclamations, which often merely repeated the prohibitions decreed by her father, Henry VIII, and sister, Mary Tudor.

Whereas it had been true that any individual could be identified as belonging to a certain class by his apparel, there was much complaint during Queen Elizabeth's reign that it was increasingly difficult to do so. Hamlet's comment, "The age is grown so picked [refined] that the toe of the peasant comes so near the heel of the courtier he galls his kibe [irritates his sore heel]," is an exaggeration, of course. The country folk were relatively unaffected by changing fashions, and few had money enough to purchase urban finery, but they supplemented "hempen homespun" with satin and velvet whenever they had the means. On the whole, fashion's influence operated much as it does today. Rural areas showed the greatest faithfulness to tried and true articles of dress and were the last to feel the impact of novelty. The clothing of the yeoman farmers and their wives, for example, was simpler and more old-fashioned than that of city craftsmen who lived nearer the center of fashion.

The passion for dress and the tendency to dress above one's station in life were the subject of frequent attacks by satirists. With the rise of Puritanism the attack became a convention of Puritan criticism. Critics of various persuasions condemned the folly of enslavement to fantastic fashion and lamented the extravagance and waste of means incurred for finery. Indeed, the Church of England itself made an effort to curb the inordinate love of clothes in an official way by including a sermon "Against Excess of Apparel" in the *Second Tome of Homilies,* which was published by government authority in 1563. The contents were intended to be preached as sermons by all parsons not licensed to preach sermons of their own composition. This particular sermon was repeated in edition after edition of the *Homilies* during the reign of Queen Elizabeth and even after James I ascended the throne. The statement therein that fashions are "at these days so outrageous that neither Almighty God, by his word, can stay our proud curiosity in the same, neither yet godly and necessary laws, made by our princes and oft repeated with the penalties, can bridle this detestable abuse" applied to the sermon itself, which had little effect on the conduct of the English audience.

Illus. 2. Queen Elizabeth in the 1570's. Her dress is handsome and bejeweled but less eccentric than it became in later years. (Portrait by an unknown artist; courtesy of the National Portrait Gallery, London.)

In their efforts to restrain extravagant dress both church and state were motivated by economic as well as ethical considerations. For example, silk, needed for the most luxurious fabrics, was not produced in England, and raw silk as well as some finished materials had to be imported from across the Channel. The cost of such luxuries sometimes caused an unfavorable trade balance and proved an economic embarrassment to the nation.

One sober observer, Philip Stubbes, complained that citizens were living beyond their incomes in a ridiculous effort to be as fine as their betters. "Everyone almost, though otherwise very poor, having scarce forty shillings of wages by the year, will be sure to have two or three pair of these silk netherstocks, or else of the finest yarn that may be got, though the price of them be a royal [approximately ten shillings] or twenty shillings, or more," he commented with disgust in his *Anatomy of Abuses* (1583). And as though that extravagance were not bad enough, over these elegant silk stockings went boot hose

of the finest cloth that may be got, yea, fine enough to make any band, ruff, or shirt needful to be worn . . . wrought all over, from the gartering place upward, with needlework, clogged with silk of all colors, fowls, beasts, and antics, portrayed all over in comely sort. So that I have known the very needlework of some one pair of these boot hose to stand, some in four pounds, six pounds, and some in ten pounds apiece. Besides this, they are made so wide to draw over all, and so long to reach up to the waist, that as little or less cloth would make one a reasonably large shirt.

Fashions, then as now, were rarely of English origin. Many observers expressed outraged national pride because English fads and fashions were derived from the Continent, and foreign travelers commented on the lack of a characteristically English style. The names of parts of the Elizabethan wardrobe indicate their foreign origins: French hose, French hood, Venetians, Spanish bonnet. The English showed less genius in designing new styles than in combining styles from many countries to create striking effects—though, indeed, the bizarre results of such combinations were the subject of much satirical comment

5

Illus. 3. A fashionable Frenchman. His short cloak has a
contrasting lining, and he wears a peasecod doublet and
Venetians. (Pietro Bertelli, *Diversarum nationum habitus*,
1594–96.)

Illus. 4. A highborn Frenchwoman wearing a Mary Stuart hood and veil stiffened behind her shoulders. Notice the point of the bodice, the sleeves that do not match the rest of the garment, and the smock which fills in the space between ruff and bodice neck. (Pietro Bertelli, *Diversarum nationum habitus,* 1594–96.)

by contemporary writers. Thomas Dekker in *The Seven Deadly Sins of London* (1606) declared that

an Englishman's suit is like a traitor's body that hath been hanged, drawn, and quartered, and is set up in several places: his codpiece is in Denmark; the color of his doublet and the belly in France; the wing and narrow sleeve in Italy; the short waist hangs over a Dutch botcher's [tailor's] stall in Utrecht; his huge slops [breeches] speak Spanish; Polonia [Poland] gives him the boots; the block for his head alters faster than the feltmaker can fit him, and thereupon we are called in scorn blockheads. And thus we that mock every nation for keeping one fashion, yet steal patches from every one of them to piece out our pride, are now laughing stocks to them because their cut so scurvily becomes us.

Portia's description of her noble English suitor is similar to other contemporary comments on the hybrid dress of fashionable young men who had traveled abroad: "I think he bought his doublet in Italy, his round hose in France, his bonnet in Germany, and his behavior everywhere."

An important factor in stimulating the English passion for dress was the enthusiasm of Queen Elizabeth herself for gorgeous clothes. Handsome costumes, besides satisfying her personal vanity, were evidence of her royalty and position and a symbol of England's power and pride. An inventory of her clothing in 1600 included almost three hundred gowns and several hundred other complete costumes, in addition to special apparel for state occasions. The Queen regarded richly ornamented stomachers, kirtles, and other articles of dress as highly acceptable gifts from her subjects. Such presents frequently appear in the annual inventories of New Year's gifts.

An indication of Elizabeth's influence on the tide of fashion in England is the extravagance of style near the end of her reign when her personal taste dictated a characteristic silhouette in which all the features of feminine attire were exaggerated almost to the point of caricature. In most of her late portraits she resembles a stuffed doll, with her tremendous ruffs, outlined against stiffened veils which are also of great size, sleeves distended, and skirts swelling out over equally big farthingales.

Stubbes aptly commented that "when they have all these goodly robes upon them, women seem to be the smallest part of themselves, not natural women, but artificial women; not women of flesh and blood, but rather puppets or mommets [dolls] of rags and cloths compact together."

Men looked equally artificial, since male and female fashion paralleled each other and corresponding parts of the dress of each swelled or shrank simultaneously. Thomas Middleton caricatured a male dandy in the early seventeenth century as follows:

. . . enters our young landlord, so metamorphosed into the shape of a French puppet that at the first we started and thought one of the baboons had marched in in man's apparel. His head was dressed up in white feathers like a shuttlecock. . . . His doublet was of a strange cut and to show the fury of his humor the collar of it rose up so high and sharp as if it would have cut his throat by daylight. His wings, according to the fashion now, were as little and diminutive as a Puritan's ruff. . . . His breeches . . . were full as deep as the middle of winter, or the roadway between London and Winchester, and so long and wide withal that I think within a twelvemonth he might very well put all his lands into them: and then you may imagine they were big enough, when they would outreach a thousand acres. . . . [He wore] a curious pair of boots of King Philip's leather, in such artificial wrinkles, sets and pleats, as if they had been starched lately and came new from the laundress'. . . . But that which struck us most into admiration, upon those fantastical boots stood such huge and wide tops, which so swallowed up his thighs, that had he sworn as other gallants did this common oath, "would I might sink as I stand," all his body might very well have sunk down and been damned in his boots. . . . Thus was our young landlord accoutered in such a strange and prodigal shape that it amounted to above two years' rent in apparel [*The Ant and the Nightingale, or Father Hubburd's Tales*, 1604].

Elizabethan men and women of the upper class dressed more for display than for comfort, and even their undergarments were designed to contribute to their appearance. The garment worn next to the skin by both sexes was a shirt, though in the case of women it was called a "smock" and was ankle-length. There is

9

Illus. 5. This falconer wears padded trunk hose with less paning than usual. His canions and the wings of his sleeves are "wrought in piccadills," and his shoes are decorated with "razing" [slashing]. (George Turberville, *The Book of Falconry,* 1575.)

some evidence that men wore drawers called "trousers"; at least Ben Jonson refers to them in *The Staple of News* (1625). Women also wore several petticoats, to help the correct hang of their kirtles, and boned underbodices, the forerunners of corsets.

Nightgowns, frequently referred to in contemporary records, were apparently dressing gowns and were often so similar to the gowns worn publicly by men and women that they could be worn abroad at the owner's discretion. Though some of the wealthy had special garments for night wear, it is very likely that most people slept naked or in their shirts or smocks, perhaps the very ones they wore every day, since standards of cleanliness were not high. Conditions in this period made personal cleanliness more difficult to achieve than a handsome appearance. Soap was generally quite coarse, though fine perfumed soaps were also available, and hot water was not a ready convenience. Of course, the fine fabrics used for the dress of the upper classes were not washable. Perfumes and sweet-smelling herbs were necessary substitutes for regular bathing and freshly laundered garments.

Elizabethan clothing was very intricate, and the amount of time that must have been consumed in donning costumes with so many independent parts to be tied or pinned together is a marvel to the modern observer. The main feminine garment usually consisted of at least two parts: bodice and skirt (known as a kirtle or petticoat). The very name "bodice," a corruption of "bodies" (a pair of bodies), indicates that it was made in two pieces. A triangular piece known as a "stomacher" formed the front section and was joined to the bodice proper at the sides by ties, hooks, or pins. The bodice was stiff, reinforced with stays and sometimes padded, and came to a point below the natural waistline.

Necklines varied; if low, the smock or a briefer garment called a "partlet" filled in the space at the top of the bodice. In Elizabeth's later years and the early years of James I's reign the bosom was often immodestly bared with the neckline of the stomacher making a downward curve. High-necked bodices had standing collars, frills, or ruffs. Feminine versions of the male

Illus. 6. The man wears a short jerkin, trunk hose with canions, and a moderate ruff. The woman, in a larger ruff, is protected from dust and damp by a "chin-clout" or muffler. Notice that the sleeves and stomacher are of different design. Her skirt appears to be shaped by a French farthingale. (John Speed, *Theatrum imperii Magnae Britanniae,* 1616.)

doublet had some popularity for a time, but these were distinguishable from the conventional bodices only by their center fastenings; even so they provoked a bellow of indignation from the satirists of the day.

Sleeves were separate and were fastened to the bodice at the shoulder line by ribbon bows or by hooks or pins concealed by decorative rolls of fabric known as "wings." The funnel-shaped sleeve common in the first half of the century went out of fashion about 1560 and sleeves thereafter might be gathered to fit closely all along the arm, tapered in a leg-of-mutton shape, or full. In any case they were tightly fitted at the wrists and finished in frills, wrist ruffs, or cuffs. Leg-of-mutton sleeves, known as "trunk" or "demi-cannon" sleeves, were shaped by stiffening or were padded. A more elaborate sleeve had a puff at the shoulder, with a change of fabric beginning just above the elbow, and might actually be made in two parts.

The skirt was not necessarily in one piece but might be opened in an inverted V in front to show a handsomely ornamented petticoat or a "forepart" of elegant design joined to the petticoat in front or fastened to the V opening.

Farthingales were usually worn to shape the full skirts. The Spanish farthingale, first introduced about the middle of the sixteenth century, became the fashion and was worn by all classes of women until about 1600. It consisted of an underskirt belled out by hoops of wood, wire, or whalebone, extending from the waist in circles which widened progressively as they neared floor level. The result was a cone-shaped skirt. The French farthingale was a padded roll worn around the hips which created a cylindrical skirt effect. The farthingale which produces the immense swell of skirts apparent in Queen Elizabeth's late portraits was a wheel or drum type. To conceal the hard line of the wheel, a "frounce" or ruffle was usually added to the skirt.

Over the kirtle and bodice a "gown" was also worn at times, mainly for added warmth or greater dignity on ceremonial occasions. This garment might be close-bodied or loose, with long sleeves or with short sleeves displaying the sleeves of the bodice

13

A Citizen *A Citizens wife*

Illus. 7. The man's gown obscures the rest of his attire, but note the hanging sleeve and his flat cap. His wife wears a large ruff and a drum or wheel farthingale. Her hair is wired into the fashionable horn-shaped headdress. (John Speed, *Theatrum imperii Magnae Britanniae,* 1616.)

14

Illus. 8. The man is booted and spurred and wears a cloak draped about him. His neckwear is a whisk or standing collar. The woman also wears a whisk, and her hair is dressed in the high coiffure fashionable after 1600. (John Speed, *Theatrum imperii Magnae Britanniae,* 1616.)

below them. Sleeves which hung loosely from the shoulder were also common. The gown opened down the front but was often buttoned or fastened by bows at least to the waist. If designed for ceremonial wear the skirt might have a train.

In cold weather cloaks or cassocks would also be necessary for outdoor wear. For traveling or riding a cloak was usually worn, and the skirt was covered with a "safeguard," an outer skirt for protection against weather and dirt. A cassock was a loose coat reaching to the hips, usually having a small collar and sometimes a hood. Another outdoor garment was the gaberdine, a long, loose coat with wide sleeves.

Besides shoes and stockings (the latter held up by garters below the knee), girdles and other accessories were indispensable to the complete costume in the highest fashion. The girdle (belt), made of silk ribbon, gold chain, or the like, followed the pointed line of the bodice, and a pomander, jewel, or muff was usually suspended from it in front. A pomander was a globular metal container for some scented concoction. Originally designed to protect the wearer against the plague, pomanders served to shield a fine lady's nose from unpleasant odors. They were ornamental as well, being made of gold or silver and often set with jewels. Half-girdles, "demi-cents," were also worn; the back section of these was more austere than the conspicuous front part. Large feather fans, of round or semicircular design, often with a small mirror in the center, were popular accessories of the noble lady, and masks were frequently carried to shield the face from the sun and the public gaze.

Both young girls and married women often went hatless, even out of doors, but the feminine head was usually covered in some fashion. Simple white coifs of linen, which hid most of the hair, were the common head covering of many women who made no pretensions to being fashionable. One type was colloquially known as "cheeks and ears" because of the way it hugged the face, with the front border forming peaks. One of the most popular head coverings was the French hood, which was introduced into England about 1530 and survived the vagaries of fashion for almost a hundred years. This was a small hood, stif-

Ein Engelische Fraw von Londen.

WAnn ein Weib gehet auß dem Hauß
Ihre Geschäfft zu richten auß/
Zu Londen vber die Strassen/
Schmücket sie sich allermassen/

Wie dises Weib gemahlet ist/
Dem an schöne gar nichts gebrist/
So ist sie sonst stattlich geziert/
Am Leib wol proportionirt. ℈

Illus. 9. An Englishwoman dressed for the street. She wears a short cape and an open ruff. The skirt which she lifts from the ground is probably a safeguard. Her girdle has a pomander and a small purse suspended from it. (Jost Amman, *Trachtenbuch,* 1586.)

Ein Fraw auß Engelland.

Ein Edelfraw in Engelland
Ist geschmücket nach ihrem Stand/
Wann sie also ist angethan/
Wie dise Figur zeiget an.

Darum hat sie ihr recht Gestalt/
Auch ihrem Mann gar wol gefalt/
Vnd wann sie ander Kleider trüg/
Ihr Mann sie zu dem Hauß außschlüg.

Illus. 10. Another Englishwoman pictured by a Dutch artist. She wears a bonnet, and the hood of her cloak hangs free behind. Her skirt demonstrates the effect of the Spanish farthingale. (Jost Amman, *Trachtenbuch,* 1586.)

fened underneath, with a curved front border and folds of material falling below the shoulders in the back. Since they were usually of dark material, these hoods were often decorated with "biliments" (borders of silk, satin, or velvet, trimmed with gold or jewels). Queen Elizabeth in 1584 received as a gift a magnificent pair of biliments of gold set with pearls, rubies, and diamonds, but humbler women would be lucky to have simple silk trimmings, or at most gold. The Mary Stuart hood was similar to the French hood but was made of sheer cloth such as lawn, trimmed with a decorative fabric, and edged with lace. The front border made a characteristic V- or U-shaped curve above the middle of the forehead. Such hoods were sometimes made of black silk and accompanied by a falling back section to indicate widowhood.

Hair nets, made of gold mesh lined with silk, of silk thread, or even of human hair, were known as "cauls" and might be worn alone to hold the back hair in a coil, or a hat might be worn with one. Women's hats copied those of men but were smaller and were usually worn at less rakish angles. Among the most stylish hats in the late sixteenth century were the taffeta pipkin and the court bonnet. The pipkin was usually trimmed with ostrich feathers and decorated with jewels and had a moderate crown and a narrow, fairly flat brim. The court bonnet was a small pillbox hat of velvet, trimmed with jewels and feathers. Both were worn with cauls. Shawls of transparent fabric known as "rails" were worn over the head and shoulders by some women.

Hair, which early in the century had been modestly drawn back and was often completely covered, during Elizabeth's reign began to be treated more like woman's crowning glory. Women often curled and dyed their hair or supplemented it with false hair. During an audience with the Queen in 1602 a Venetian envoy's observant eye noted her "hair . . . of a light color never made by nature." There are many other comments similar to Shakespeare's reference to "crisped, snaky golden locks . . . often known to be the dowry of a second head." False hair was often needed for the elaborate headdresses which de-

Illus. 11. Queen Elizabeth dressed in the fashion of her later years. She wears a wired headrail decorated with pearls and jewels and a large drum farthingale. Notice the stiffness of her sleeves and the hanging sleeves which simulate a gown. (Portrait by an unknown artist, 1592; courtesy of the National Portrait Gallery, London.)

veloped in the late sixteenth century, and whole wigs might be used. An Elizabethan woman could manage more easily the pearl strands and other ornaments if the whole coiffure was made on a wig stand. To set off the head, wired headrails of gauze were sometimes worn. Those worn by Queen Elizabeth arched in stiffened curves behind her head and shoulders and were generously trimmed with pearls.

Variety in materials, color, and ornaments characterized the Elizabethan woman's outer garments. Bodice and kirtle as often as not were of different fabrics. Sleeves might match some other garment, but not necessarily, and the forepart of the kirtle offered another opportunity for variety. Any part of the costume was likely to be decorated with braid, embroidery, pinking (pricking in patterns), slashing, or puffing, or it might be encrusted with pearls, jewels, or spangles or trimmed with lace or artificial flowers. The smock was usually embroidered and frilled at the neck. Partlets to fill in the top of the bodice were often as ornate.

Although all classes in the Elizabethan period began to dress better, for obvious reasons the clothing of wealthy and prominent people is more fully described and illustrated than that of humble folk. Most generalizations therefore, apply to people in court circles or to those exposed to the influence of the court. Conservative gentlewomen and the wives of prosperous merchants and officials had taffeta, satin, and velvet in their wardrobes, but on the whole their garments were more sober than those of court ladies, and durability was a factor to be considered in the fashioning of their apparel. Women of yeoman stock largely confined their selection of clothing to worsted, russet, and other nonluxurious woolens, though they might have velvet trim on their best kirtles and gowns. Clothing was sufficiently valued to be included as special bequests to friends and relatives when wills were made, especially garments "guarded" with velvet or trimmed with gold lace.

The favorite materials among the wealthy were silk, taffeta, velvet, and brocade. Bright colors were favored, particularly reds (Bristol red, flame, lusty gallant, sanguine, carnation, gin-

Illus. 12. The plain dress of unpretentious English folk is shown in this picture. The man wears a flat cap and a gown over a jerkin. The small frills showing above the collar of his jerkin and the bodice of the woman's dress later developed into the ruff. The soft folds of the woman's skirt probably indicate that she wears no farthingale. The child at the left still wears skirts, as did most children of both sexes. (*The Whole Book of Psalms in Four Parts,* 1563.)

gerline, maiden's blush, scarlet) and oranges (tawny, orange-tawny, horseflesh color [bronze]). Black set off by silver or gold was also frequently worn, and white was popular at court. Color symbolism was very important to the Elizabethans. Blue, symbolizing constancy, was conventionally associated with serving-men and apprentices, and because of this men and women of higher rank avoided shades of true blue, though they wore watchet (light blue with a greenish tinge) and azure (a lapis lazuli blue).

Elizabethan women delighted in gorgeous dress. But despite the richness of their attire, men frequently outshone them in complexity of costume and the variety of cuts that contemporary fashion provided. The capriciousness of masculine taste was ridiculed by Andrew Boorde in 1548 in his *First Book of the Introduction of Knowledge* by a woodcut of a man clothed only in a plumed hat and a breechclout, holding cloth and shears, with the explanatory verse:

> I am an Englishman, and naked I stand here
> Musing in my mind what raiment I shall wear,
> For now I will wear this, and now I will wear that;
> Now I will wear I cannot tell what.

The costume corresponding to a twentieth-century suit was basically doublet and hose, "hose" being composed of breeches and stockings made separately but sometimes sewn together. Under the doublet a shirt was worn and perhaps a waistcoat; the latter was an underdoublet usually padded and probably worn for added warmth. If the breeches were short, they might be supplemented by "canions," close-fitting cylinders of cloth resembling the knee breeches of a later period. Over the doublet a jerkin was also worn at times. The jerkin was often sleeveless and was a somewhat looser garment than the doublet, though following the same cut.

The doublet was a jacket, cut to fit the torso, though during most of the sixteenth century its waistline came to a point below the natural waistline. The skirts became so abbreviated in the late sixteenth century that they were mere borders just below

Within the engraving:

Are to be fould in Popes head Alley at the white horse
by Iohn Sudbury and George Humble

R. Elstrake
fculp.

The most illustrious Prince Henry, Lord Darnly, King of Scotland, father
to our Soueraygne lord King Iames. He died at the age of 21. 1567.

The most excellent Princesse Marie Queene of Scotland, mother to our Soue
raygne lord King Iames. She died. 1586. and intombed at Westminster

Illus. 13. Mary Queen of Scots and her second husband, Lord Darnley. Mary wears an
open ruff edged with lace, the hood to which she gave her name, and a wired headrail.
Her kirtle is open to show an ornate forepart, and her jeweled girdle ends in a large
jewel. Lord Darnley wears typical, paned trunk hose and a cloak draped in a customary negligent manner. He holds a baton resting against his right hip. Notice the
ribbon bows on his flat-heeled shoes and the ribboned garters. (An engraving by
Renold Elstracke, executed *ca.* 1604.)

24

the girdle line, but they still served to conceal the "points" which tied doublet and hose together. The front opening was fastened with decorative buttons or loops or tied with points. Stiffening and padding were usual, and many an Elizabethan gallant had, instead of padded shoulders, a padded chest. A Dutch fashion known as a peasecod belly became popular in the last quarter of the sixteenth century, and in consequence doublets were often so heavily padded near the point that they bulged and drooped below the girdle. Philip Stubbes describes them, perhaps exaggeratedly, as stuffed with four to six pounds of bombast.

Doublets sometimes had high standing collars, often finished with stiff tabs called "piccadills" to support the ruffs. The shirt collar was sometimes pulled over the doublet collar and spread below the ruff. Late in the century when deep collars called "falling bands" were more common, the neckline became flatter. The sleeves were separate and laced or hooked to the doublet, with the joint concealed by wings, often "wrought in piccadills." Sleeve styles were similar to those of women's dress.

Breeches generally took the form of "trunk hose"; these were puffed, often stuffed, rounded breeches reaching to mid-thigh, though the length varied greatly, some being almost concealed by the skirts of the doublet. The fabric of trunk hose was usually "paned"; that is, vertical strips of one fabric alternated with strips of another of a different pattern or color. "Venetians" were chiefly distinguished by their length, coming just below the knee, and were often padded to give a voluminous effect. These were not necessarily paned like trunk hose. "Galligaskins" were apparently similar to Venetians, but Stubbes differentiates between them, describing "gally-hosen" as coming only to the knee and Venetians below. "Open hose" were breeches that hung loose below the knee. They were cut straight across and were usually braided at the sides. This style made its appearance late in the sixteenth century and never became very popular until the mid-seventeenth century.

Over the doublet, and possibly over a jerkin as well, cloaks of various lengths were worn. Short cloaks were frequently

Illus. 14. The falconer wears padded Venetians. His matching doublet and hose are slashed, as are the wings of his doublet. The other two men are wearing trunk hose, and the one in the foreground also wears canions and garters. (George Turberville, *The Book of Falconry,* 1575.)

made to match the trunk hose as a part of the ensemble and might be worn indoors as well as out. Three-quarter-length capes with sleeves, called "mandilions," were dashing versions of the cloak. Stylish gallants affected a fantastic mode of wearing mandilions turned around sideways so that the sleeves hung down in front and behind. Mandilions worn in this way were said to be "Collie-Westonward." The sleeves of these garments were so little used that tailors eventually made mock sleeves that could not be worn.

A long open-front gown over other clothing was worn by some men, but chiefly older men, particularly officials. Short gowns were popular with stylish young men until about 1570. Cassocks and gaberdines were also worn for warmth outdoors.

Men's clothing, like that of women, was gorgeous with color and ornamentation. The many parts of male attire contributed to the ornate and colorful effect of the ensemble. Trunk hose need not match the doublet, canions could be of another fabric or design, and the netherstocks might be still different. Ensembles of matching doublet and hose were not unknown, however.

The fashionable gallant's doublet and hose were commonly made of satin, taffeta, velvet, or some other rich fabric; they were decorated with slashing, pinking, embroidery, or any of the other types of ornamentation used on feminine apparel. Colored lining, or a colored shirt, might be drawn through slashes in puffs to ornament the doublet and sleeves. Cloaks and gowns were richly trimmed with fur or gold braid, and the stockings might be patterned or clocked in silver or gold. Men were as lavish as women in the wearing of jewelry, even to the wearing of earrings, though men usually wore a ring in only one ear at a time. Even the shirt, which was politely concealed under the doublet except for the collar, might be elaborately embroidered, perhaps with "black work," in which English embroiderers excelled.

Men of modest station dressed in more somber colors and fabrics of greater durability than fashionable men of higher rank. Yeomen might have in their wardrobes no fabric richer

Illus. 15. William Herbert, earl of Pembroke. He wears a Vandyke beard and an earring in the right ear. Notice the ring suspended from his bandstrings, the lace-edged falling band, and the decorative wing to his sleeve. (Engraving after a portrait by Daniel Mytens, *ca.* 1620.)

Illus. 16. Robert Devereux, earl of Essex. He wears a lace ruff with "disordered sets," a peasecod doublet, and brief, paned trunk hose with canions. (Engraving after a portrait by Nicholas Hilliard [n.d.].)

than fustian, an inexpensive substitute for velvet made of cotton or flax and wool. The traditional dress of countrymen is indicated in two quotations from Robert Greene. He describes "a plain country fellow well and cleanly appareled, either in a coat of homespun russet, or of frieze [a sturdy woolen with a heavy nap]" (A Notable Discovery of Cozenage, 1591). Elsewhere referring to a character in a pastoral, he pictures him as "tired in his russet jacket, his red sleeves of chamlet [a fine silk], his blue bonnet, and his round slop of country cloth" (Menaphon, 1589). Russet is not a color here but the name of a coarse woolen which varied in color from natural to reddish-brown.

Men wore hats even indoors, though they were doffed in the presence of royalty or as a courtesy to others of high degree. Male headgear hugged the head until the 1570's, when hats with high crowns became increasingly fashionable. The "copintank" or "copotain" hat, described by Stubbes as "sharp on the crown, perking up like a sphere or shaft of a steeple," was particularly popular. Feathers and jewels were typical ornaments. A small, flat cap like a beret with a narrow brim continued to be worn by craftsmen and many other citizens of London and was famous as the "City Flat Cap." This cap was almost a badge of London residence. With the object of assisting local industry, an Act of Parliament in 1571 required all citizens with the exception of the nobility, gentry, and officeholders to wear on Sundays and holidays knitted caps of wool manufactured in England. These "statute caps" were worn by many until the statute was repealed in 1597.

Masculine hair styles varied greatly. Sometimes the hair was cut closely at the sides, but it could be brushed up and held with gum, or it might be curled all over the head. From 1590 onward, long hair was more common and it was often worn curling to the shoulders, perhaps with a long curl at the left side called a "lovelock." Men in this period did not disdain to have their hair curled by artificial means if necessary. Most men also wore beards of a variety of cuts, ranging from a Vandyke style to a spade or full shape. Mustaches were an inevitable accompaniment but were rarely seen without beards.

Illus. 17. Robert Dudley, earl of Leicester. His costume includes a bonnet, a falling collar with matching cuffs, a short gown with fur facing, and paned trunk hose. The chain he wears is the collar of the Order of the Garter. (Engraving by Robert Cooper after the original in the collection of the Marquis of Salisbury.)

Illus. 18. Francis Bacon wearing a long gown with hanging sleeves, decorated with braid. His neckwear is a falling band of lace. (After a portrait from the studio of Paul van Somer.)

Shoes for men and women were similar. They were made of many materials, usually luxurious ones: Spanish leather, called "cordwain" (Cordovan), silk, brocade, or velvet. In the sixteenth century they were generally flat-heeled, but toward the end of the period small heels began to appear. Scuffs known as "pantofles" were introduced about 1570 for the protection of dainty footgear outdoors, but the prevailing taste for luxury was such that the pantofles themselves soon were made of rich fabrics and in time they retreated indoors for use as house slippers. Cork soles raised the foot in pantofles from close contact with the ground, and some pantofles had excessively thick soles, a concession to fashion rather than utility. Shoes of stouter leather were also used for outdoor wear. Pattens, which had raised soles or were elevated from the ground by a ring of metal, were worn over elegant footgear to keep them from the mud. Boots, utilitarian or elegant, were also common for masculine wear.

Among other accessories of the male costume were gloves, sometimes perfumed, purses, worn slung from the belt or carried in the sleeve or hose, and fans, carried only by the more effeminate dandies. Swords or rapiers, and sometimes daggers, slung on chains or belts of elaborate design, were worn by many men. Steel collars, called "gorgets," actually a part of armor, were sometimes worn with ordinary civilian dress.

An extravagance of both masculine and feminine dress, and a theme for much satirical comment, was the ruff, which had grown to great size by the time Elizabeth began her reign in 1558. Starch was introduced into England about 1560, and its use made possible even larger and stiffer ruffs. Despite her own use of wide ruffs, Queen Elizabeth objected to the spread of the fashion, and her sumptuary statute of 1580 forbade the wearing of neckwear larger than a certain size. The citizens of London were ordered to enforce the observance of this restriction, and members of the Ironmongers' and Grocers' companies were stationed at Bishopsgate in London from morning till evening to stop any passerby entering the city with "monstrous ruffs" or swords or cloaks of excessive length. If offenders re-

Illus. 19. Anne of Denmark, wife of James I. Her bodice shows the extreme decolletage popular with stylish women. She wears a wired collar and a frounced skirt. Notice the loveknots on her sleeve and at the edge of her bodice, and the deep lace cuffs. (Engraving by Simon van de Passe, 1616.)

fused to reform their costume, they were subject to arrest. Despite the efforts to prohibit large ruffs, according to Stubbes, writing in 1583, they often measured nine inches or more from inner to outer edge.

Ruffs were shaped into tubular pleats by means of tools made of wood or bone called "setting sticks," but in the 1570's "poking sticks" of steel were introduced. The instruments were used in the same way as a curling iron on human hair. A newly laundered ruff or "band" was placed in a round box for protection; from this we get the expression "just stepped out of a bandbox" to indicate sartorial perfection. Despite elaborate efforts to shape and stiffen ruffs, they did not withstand bad weather gracefully, and Stubbes pictures them as going "flip-flap in the wind like rags flying abroad." The larger ruffs required wired props called "supportasses" to hold them erect. The open ruffs popular after 1570 were pinned to "rebatos," wired frames covered with linen.

Though neckwear was usually white, yellow ruffs and cuffs had a vogue for a time after Mrs. Turner, a dressmaker for the court during James I's time, brought from France the method of making yellow starch. Mrs. Turner was involved in the notorious Overbury poisoning case and was executed in 1615 for her part in it. To bring ridicule upon the fad of wearing yellow ruffs, which disgusted King James, Chief Justice Coke ordered that Mrs. Turner be sent to the gallows wearing the detested yellow bands. But apparently yellow retained some popularity, for there are references to yellow bands in the 1620's.

James I's accession to the throne in 1603 saw no immediate or drastic change in English style, but dress gradually assumed greater freedom in comparison with the stiffness that developed during Elizabeth's long reign. Ruffs were replaced by "whisks," standing collars supported by piccadills; a familiar example is the collar in the Droeshout engraving of William Shakespeare on the title-page of the First Folio edition of his plays.

Women's necklines became lower than before, frequently having only a narrow lace edging at the bosom without either ruff or collar. Both men and women wore their hair longer and allowed it to flow in curls. Farthingales narrowed and in time disappeared. Numerous petticoats provided a softer fullness for the skirts. The male doublet acquired a more natural waistline, and trunk hose were replaced by full, loose-fitting breeches without padding. Boots became more and more common with men of every class. Shoes acquired heels and were decorated with large rosettes. In general, both male and female dress drifted toward the "Cavalier" costume associated with the mid-seventeenth century.

English men and women of both the Elizabethan and Jacobean periods made dressing an art when their means permitted it. Though colors may have been brighter than is customary in modern dress, particularly masculine dress, the use of color was not always gaudy. Contemporary documents list subtle combinations such as peach-color cloth of silver, lined with ash-color unshorn velvet. Tasteful elegance was the ideal of the great, and the more sophisticated apparently realized that black and white, silver and gold, and similar combinations of contrasting colors could be used for costumes with striking effects, as is demonstrated by the costumes worn in many portraits of great personages including Sir Walter Raleigh, the Earl of Essex, the Earl of Leicester, Sir Christopher Hatton, and Queen Elizabeth herself. Indeed, the portrait of Raleigh in the National Portrait Gallery, in which he wears white silk and black velvet, decorated with silver, represents the very model of a fine Elizabethan gentleman at his handsomest.

Illus. 20. Mary Queen of Scots, whose taste for drama often dictated black and white dress. (Painting attributed to P. Oudry, 1578; courtesy of the National Portrait Gallery, London.)

Illus. 21. Sir Walter Raleigh in black and silver. (Portrait by an unknown artist, 1588; courtesy of the National Portrait Gallery, London.)

SUGGESTED READING

The literature of the period is rich in references to contemporary clothing. An introduction to the subject will be found in the chapter on costume in Volume II of *Shakespeare's England* (2 vols., Oxford, 1916). Contemporary portraits constitute the most reliable guides to what English dress actually looked like.

An excellent general discussion is contained in the volume by Graham Reynolds in the series "Costume of the Western World," *Elizabethan and Jacobean, 1558–1625* (London, 1951), illustrated by carefully chosen contemporary portraits, some in color. Details of every part of male and female dress are described, with line illustrations taken from contemporary portraits and memorial brasses, in C. Willett and Phillis Cunnington, *Handbook of English Costume in the Sixteenth Century* (London, 1954) and *Handbook of English Costume in the Seventeenth Century* (London, 1955). Though it is poorly illustrated, much useful information about fabrics, colors (including color symbolism), and styles is given in M. Channing Linthicum, *Costume in the Drama of Shakespeare and His Contemporaries* (Oxford, 1936). Both the Cunningtons and Miss Linthicum give many quotations from contemporary documents to amplify their texts.

Information about undergarments is scanty, but C. Willett and Phillis Cunnington, *The History of Underclothes* (London, 1951) provides the most complete discussion of this aspect of the dress of Shakespeare's age.

Herbert Norris, *Costume and Fashion, Vol. III, The XVIth Century* (London, 1938) has many illustrations and is particularly good for pictures and discussion of details such as embroidery.

F. M. Kelly, *Shakesperian Costume for Stage and Screen* (London, 1938) is designed to foster accurate reproduction of the dress of this period for theatrical purposes and includes discussions of costuming most of the plays of Shakespeare. Details of costume are illustrated by line drawings after contemporary illustrations.

Also useful are F. M. Kelly and Randolph Schwabe, *Historic Costume, 1490–1790* (London, 1925) and Millia Davenport, *The Book of Costume* (2 vols., New York, 1948; 2 vols. in 1, New York, 1956), copiously illustrated with contemporary portraits, English and Continental, which provide an opportunity to compare English dress with that of other countries.

Iris Brooke, *A History of English Costume* (London, 1937), *English Costume in the Age of Elizabeth. The Sixteenth Century* (London, 1938), and *English Costume in the Seventeenth Century* (London, 1934), all illustrated by the author, are less accurate and should be used with care.

Elizabethan embroidery, which played such a large part in the decoration of dress, is pictured with a brief discussion in the Victoria and Albert Museum's Small Picture Book No. 5, *Elizabethan Embroidery* (1948 and 1956).

Two older standard works, Joseph Strutt, *A Complete View of the Dress and Habits of the People of England* (2 vols., London, 1796–1799) and J. R. Planché, *History of British Costume from the Earliest Period to the Close of the Eighteenth Century* (London, 1847), are rather outdated.